Table Of Contents

Chapter 1: Mastering the Game of Wealth

Chapter 2: No One is born with the Knowledge of Becoming Rich

Chapter 3: The Mindset of the Rich

Chapter 4: Rich People always think Northward

Chapter 5: Unshackle your Thoughts from your Circumstances

Chapter 6: Make Friends with Money

Chapter 7: God wants us to be Rich

Chapter 8: The Rich make Opportunities knock at their Door

Chapter 9: Giving Back

Chapter 10: Putting your Best Foot Forward

Introduction

What is it that makes some people richer and richer and others poorer and poorer? Who has decreed that this divide should exist in our world? Is there any way in which the line can be crossed, and the "have-nots" can make their place among the privileged "haves"?

Can you make the jump from being the person who has to think about paying the next electricity bill to being the person who thinks about owning the electricity grid for the state?

Yes you can. The answer lies in the mind.

The answer lies in understanding the wealth that resides within the mind of each and every one of us.

Chapter 1: Mastering the Game of Wealth

Earning money is a game. The only thing is that some people hold the strings while others are the puppets. The fun part is that you can decide which side of the game you want to be on – the puppeteer or the puppet.

Mastering the Game of Wealth

No one on this planet was born lucky. Everyone 'lucky' that you can think of – the richest people on the planet probably – weren't born lucky. Agreed that some of these people were born to rich families and in rich homes, but we all know that that is not enough to make things happen.

The fact is that these people have mastered the game of wealth later on in their lives. They may or may not have been born with the money, but they have learnt how to play the money game.

People speak a lot about the game of wealth without really knowing what it means. In life, we need to put in something to get something. Even with money it is like that. If you want to make money, you need to put in something. This may be a financial investment or it could be some other kind of investment such as an investment of time or effort or a particular talent or intelligence, etc. But the fact is that something needs to be invested.

Chapter 2: Rich Knowledge

However, there is a lot of difference in what people invest. Some people might invest a lot but receive very little, while there are also people who invest almost No One is born with the Knowledge of Becoming Rich nothing but get a lot. These people know how to make the most of what they have. They know how to put in almost nothing and get what most people in the world would be in awe of. These are the people who have mastered the game of wealth.

The best thing is that the game of wealth is not inaccessible and nor is it unattainable. Anyone can attune him- or herself to become a master at this game. Whatever their current situation is, they can veer their lives in the direction of big money. You can do it too. What you need is the right mindset, the right approach and a few other things. This is where you begin.

The knowledge of becoming rich comes on later in life. This is how you can acquire your education in this area.

No One is born with the Knowledge of Becoming Rich

We have already stated how people are never born with their richness. They might be born into richness, but this richness is not theirs. If they have to make it their own, they have to work for it.

It is a fact that a rich man will be just as concerned about his son as a poor man would be. They would both think how their sons would manage things when they grew older. The bottom line here is – Every man has to work towards richness. They are not born with the knowledge.

Think about one of the richest men of our times – Bill Gates. The son of a humble attorney and a schoolteacher today has a net worth of 40 billion dollars, making him the richest businessman in the world. All his wealth has come from a single source – Microsoft –, which in itself is one of the most influential companies of the world in any age and period.

Do you think Bill Gates was educated differently from the rest of us? Was he a brighter kid than all the rest? In fact, no. Yes, he did become a student at Harvard, but he left his education midway in order to pursue his business (which became Microsoft). Actually, his teacher once challenged him for his lackadaisical nature, when he retorted that he would earn his first million before he hit 20 years of age. Well, Bill Gates earned his first billion before he reached 21 years of age.

So what set him apart? One of the things that made him different at that time was that he knew what he wanted to do. He did not allow the razzle-dazzle of his big- name university faze him. He kept his focus on what drove him. He liaised with the right people; people who he knew could take him forward and whom he could take forward in the process too. He remained truthful to himself about his financial position and he promised to himself to do better.

But, most importantly, Bill Gates did not actively think about money!

He instead thought about the quality of his product. He asked himself repeatedly, "Is what I am providing going to do anything for the world?" That is what set him apart. We usually think, "Will this make a profit for me?" while the people who attain richness think, "Will this profit the world?"

And this knowledge does not come at birth. You learn this as you grow, just as you learn various other things. You learn that richness does not come by thinking about money; in fact, that has the opposite effect.

The thing to remember here is that no one is born with the knowledge of becoming rich. You learn that as you grow, in the same manner as you learn so many other things. But what really makes you rich is implementing this knowledge at the right moment in your life.

Chapter 3: The Mindset of the Rich

The rich mind does think differently than the middleclass mind. Yes, it is true that richness dwells in the mind and not in the bank balance.

The Mindset of the Rich

It is quite true that the rich mind thinks differently. They have a much different way of thinking from the so-called middleclass and the poor person's mind. We have already taken a glimpse into that. The rich person's mind thinks more about providing quality than about earning their own profit. They think about how their products benefit society. This is what makes people believe in what they give and buy those things. Making people buy their product is one of the least things in the rich person's mind.

There are other traits that typify the rich person's mind. One of these is the leadership quality that they have. Look around – all rich men and women of the world today are leaders in some way or the other. Most of them are heads of state or hold some other such position of power. A lot of them are businessmen and businesswomen who command about a hundred people each day. Several of them are celebrities in the world of movies and sport; even these people are leaders in their own right because they rule the world to which they belong.

The other quality is charisma. Without that, richness does not befit a person. The person must be able to carry his or her richness. They must be able to exude the confidence from being rich. They need to have a positive attitude. What is the purpose of being rich if you are worried about your finances anyway?

Rich people also think about benevolence and charity. Every

person that is rich is involved with a lot of different causes; most of them have set up NGOs and other such organizations to benefit the masses. This shows their social streak. After all, all rich men and women arise from an innate desire to do good for the society, whether that is through their commercial products or through their charitable deeds.

To be a rich person, you need to begin thinking like one. This is where you have to begin changing your personality. Read biographies of the top rich people of the world and see what you can take from this study.

Chapter 4: Rich People always think Northward

People who have reached their pinnacles of success in our present world have one thing in common – they have never thought about anything less than the best.

Rich People always think Northward

One common trait that you will find about the rich people in the world today or at any time is that they never think small. Rich people tend to think about the largest, the biggest, the grandest, the most opulent and so on. Not just that, they carry in them a supreme confidence that they will achieve what they think. This is what sets them apart. Rich people always look at the north, the very zenith of achievement.

If you want to acquire richness, you have to definitely emulate this way of thinking. You have to align your mind's compass northward too. You have to dream big; you have to think that you can achieve what you are setting your mind to. Suppose that your life's ambition is to own a chain of five star hotels, but you don't even have proper money for your room rent right now. Should you just brush this ambition to the deepest recesses of your mind, telling yourself that you can never achieve it?

Not at all! Instead, you have to work in yourself the confidence that you can achieve. You have to think that this will happen. When you think that way – when your work in yourself the absolute faith that this can happen – it will certainly happen.

Basically, the Law Of Attraction states that if you want to achieve something and if your desire for that is most intense, then the fates itself will align themselves in such a way that you get what you hanker for.

Think there's no truth in this? Well, consider it again! Let's take the hotel ambition example. Even if you are living in a rented room right now, if you have a burning desire for achieving your hotels one day, and if you spend every waking moment thinking about it and every sleeping moment dreaming about it, then you are automatically going to take steps in the direction of fulfilling your ambition. Every step that you take will be a step in that direction, whether it is saving a $100 a week or whether it is seeking financial assistance from banks some years down the line. If your ambition is overwhelming, you are going to do stuff to make it happen.

It works. Rich people have proved that this kind of ambitious thinking works. Do you think Donald Trump would have been the conglomerate he is today if he had been happy with his first solitary business? Do you think Bill Gates would have been the richest person in the world today if he had stayed put with the successful BASIC software he designed with Paul Allen? Not a bit. It is because these people thought northward and kept thinking that way that they got the success they always dreamt of.

Chapter 5: Unshackle your Thoughts from your Circumstances

Most times, you are your own enemy. You get in the way of making yourself rich. You need to vanquish yourself to an extent to get those riches.

Unshackle your Thoughts from your Circumstances

Maybe you have a very strong desire of becoming one of the richest people the world has seen but probably you are getting in the way of yourself. Have you ever thought along the following lines: -

> → € "How can I ever reach the success these Forbes people have reached?"

> → € "How can I, a man with a $500 wage, become a millionaire?"

> → € "I cannot even dream of becoming rich because no one in my family has ever been rich."

> → € "I am not able to pay even my rent. How can I buy a luxury yacht?" See what you are doing? You are letting yourself get in your way. You are not unleashing your full potential just because you think you cannot do it. You have some circumstances in life – everyone has – which you think will prevent you from getting at all those riches we are speaking about. But if you read biographies of the richest people in the world today, you will find that a very significant amount of them have risen from slums, garbage dumps, ghettos, back alleys and so on. A lot of them haven't had money to eat once. A lot of their families haven't seen a $100 together except at Christmas. Do you still think you cannot do it? Remember that no one is born into richness – not even

the kids of the richest people today. Everyone has to live and learn how to sustain their wealth or to how to earn it. That is the reason you have to free yourself from yourself. Stop thinking that you cannot achieve just because you are of a different religion, a different color, a different social background, different educational qualification, a physical or mental challenge or whatever. History has proved time and again that adversity breeds prosperity. You could be the next rags- to- riches story on the Forbes. Do you have your mind set on becoming rich? Do you have that one talent you think the world really wants? Are you already a small name in your small market? Are you confident of becoming rich? If yes, then you have to definitely make the effort. Remember that richness can come from anywhere.

Chapter 6: Make Friends with Money

Money is probably the worst reputed thing in our world. But the fact is, money makes the world go round.

Make Friends with Money

How many times have you heard negative associations with money in our common day language? Consider these…

- ✓ *If you have money, you become greedy.*
- ✓ *Wants are never satiated.*
- ✓ *Money doesn't grow on trees.*
- ✓ *No gains without pains.*
- ✓ *Money makes false friends.*

This is our everyday language. But, looking at these expressions, it does seem that money is a very bad thing, doesn't it? No one would have a positive impression of money if they were educated with these dictums.

In fact, this is the reason why more than half the people of the world are bogged down by problems concerning money. Why, we should say the ratio of people with financial problems must be even larger than that! We learn such negative associations about money that we begin feeling that money is a very bad thing.

Our parents, teachers, religious preachers, spiritual gurus, everyone tell us that money is a very bad thing to have. But then even these people are in the game for the money, right? We develop such a bad perspective about money from our early childhood from these people that throughout life we do not consider it favorably. And when we grow up, we pass on this mantle of hatred toward money to our children and they grow up hating it too.

The result – one financially limited generation gives birth to another.

We need to stop this cycle right now. We need to remove this highly incorrect view about money that we are fed on. We have to make friends with money.

Money is actually what sustains economic life on this earth. Without it, not a single button could change hands. We have built the world on the base of money and now there's no way we can run away from it.

Do not regard money as your enemy. This is what defeatists do. These are the people who haven't earned money in their lives or probably have earned so much that they don't care whether others do or not.

You have to improve your own situation. It is time you made friends with money.

Chapter 7: God wants us to be Rich

If money were evil, why do we equate God with abundance?

God wants us to be Rich

Throughout the Book of Genesis, we have several examples that God loves abundance. The very Garden of Eden that God built was the epitome of overabundance. Everything was plentiful for Man in that garden and God asked us to freely peruse it.

Our sinful deeds got us banished from the Garden of Eden, but that did not deter God from taking us to the path of richness. If you read through the stories of Abraham, Noah, Moses and David, you see how God wanted people to be rich. He even gifted them with things in return of their good deeds. God rewarded Man with riches. Then, can our God be against us becoming rich?

Some people with vested interest twist religion. They speak about God being against riches. They even go so far as to say that hoarding money is going against the Word of God. Well, if that were the case, why do we always claim that God is the richest and most abundant entity in the Universe?

The fact is that God loves people being charitable. And charity comes automatically if you are rich. God understands that Man needs to be happy to be benevolent. Only when Man can fill his own cup can he allow it to overflow to others. If God has made Man completely in His image, and if God is exceedingly rich, wouldn't He want Man to be likewise too?

We have been handed down a very warped view about religion as regards money. For us, it is important to discard this false cloak we have been asked to wear and see things as they are. Perhaps, the Reformation movement was not complete. They should have made people understand that God is not against earning money, but that He is against using money in the wrong way.

If you start thinking that our God wants us to become rich, you will see that you automatically begin taking significant steps toward becoming rich.

Chapter 8: The Rich make Opportunities Knock

Opportunities don't come your way all the time. You know that. But with the rich, this adage doesn't work. A truly successful man is a person who can sniff out an opportunity and realize its potential. Yes, opportunities do knock more than twice at a successful person's door.

The Rich make Opportunities knock at their Door

Opportunities don't knock twice. How many times have you heard it said? But, do you really think this adage is true?

The fact of the matter is that you *can* make opportunities knock at your door as many times as you want. Haven't you ever heard of people who have become successful, then fizzled out, and then resurged to become better than before? It happens all the time around us. Opportunities don't come by only once. However, to make them come to you over and over again, you need some skills.

Understanding Opportunities

Firstly, you must understand what an 'opportunity' means. Just like God, opportunities come in various shapes and sizes too. A simple email address could be your opportunity. A visiting card lying on your desk unclaimed could be your opportunity. An evening at the mall could be your opportunity because you might meet someone special. The thing is, you should not play down anything. Anything can turn your life for the better.

Recall Value

Sometimes, you need to go back and think. You have to remember things. When you meet a familiar face suddenly on the road, if you are able to immediately place them, they might be so impressed with you that they invite you for a business deal. A good memory always helps. You will see that all people at the helm have great memories. Get into some memory building exercises if you aren't gifted with a natural elephantine memory.

Never Saying "Die"

Most people who meet with failure once are liable to think that they will never succeed again. To add to that, there are several detractors all around them who always tell they won't be able to rise again. However, it is very important that you don't bow down to what others think. You have to be sure that a new opportunity will be found and you will become better.

Never stop looking for Opportunities

Usually, when someone finds that they have found something good, they stop looking for anything else. Probably, you are already into a successful business venture. When such a situation is present, you are quite unlikely to look at anything else closely. However, you must make sure that you don't stop looking. Maybe, a new opportunity will come your way and taking it up can make you richer than you were before. Take a look at Donald Trump, or any successful businessperson for that matter. They already have their own highly powerful businesses. But, does that stop them from looking at other avenues? They are always diversifying, and giving their new opportunities the same energy that they gave their first one.

These four qualities ensure that the opportunities never stop coming to you. You gain from strength to strength. This is what pushes you on.

Chapter 9: Giving Back

You need to give back if you need to get more. This is the fundamental law of nature. It doesn't work any other way.

Giving Back

We see this everywhere around us. On the farm, for example. When the farmer harvests his crop, he sows back some of the seeds into the farm. These seeds will help him get more crop. You see what is happening – The farmer is giving back something of what he gets. This is what ensures that he gets more.

Look at Bill Gates himself. He is the founder of one of the largest charitable organizations in the world, the Bill and Melinda Gates Foundation. This institution works in several countries, all the countries that he has made his riches from. He is giving back. When he does that, people feel good about him. This helps him consolidate his position. Of course, that's not his idea when he is doing good for others, but that's the way it works, isn't it?

Take a look at any celebrity, any industrialist, anybody who is doing well. In their own way, everyone is contributing to some cause or the other.

Why are they doing that? Why don't they just hoard all the wealth that they have got and forget about the world? That's because when you become rich, you hear that deep inner voice telling you to give back. When you do, you feel good about it. You see the abundance flowing. You gain strength from the feeling that you have given something back to the people who have helped make you rich.

Hoarding is the mentality of the poor. Giving back is the mentality of the rich.

When you give back, you can associate with people who could help you become stronger. This always works. In this world, magnanimity is the route to success.

Chapter 10: Putting your Best Foot Forward

A mindset of being rich has been portrayed by the media as a villainous mindset. Why is that? Does the incessant desire to become rich mean that you are evil?

Putting your Best Foot Forward

Quite often, we have seen people being spoken ill about because they have an unwavering desire to become rich. "Money is all that is on his mind," "He will do anything for money,"… such are the talks we hear about them. That might deter some of us from entering into moneymaking ventures. Some of us get the impression that it is a horrible thing to think about money.

However, there is something you must know – It is not making money that is bad. It is the way some people do it that's bad.

You have to become rich. But at the same time you have to see what costs you have to pay for it. Are you becoming rich at the expense of spending time with your family members? Are you becoming rich putting some innocent people at stake? If you are doing that, you are evil. But if you are earning money through righteous ways and then helping other people do that too, then you are doing it the right way. This is the way you earn money and make sure you sustain it too.

How does that happen? That happens when you put your best foot forward. Put your best effort and you will see that it will work your way and you will even feel good about earning your money. There are two ways to earn money – the evil way and the honest way where you show people your best talents. The second way always works, and it does much better if you can enlist other people into your act.

Sharpen yourself. Make yourself stronger. When people see you have talents that they don't, or you have knowledge that you don't, they will flock around you. And they won't mind making you rich in the process.

You are being morally correct, you are being benevolent and you are getting rich. Isn't that the way everyone wants richness to come to them?

That is when you really enjoy that you have the capacity to spend – when you know that you have made a hundred other people able to spend too.

Conclusion

Becoming rich is a process, it is not a phenomenon. You have to constantly strive to make it happen; nobody is born into richness.

You have with you now the knowledge to go about this process the right way. Good luck!

Notes